SUMAK KAUSAY (GOOD LIVING)
FOR A FLOURISHING AUTISM

Contexts and meanings of the experience from the Andean Global South

Coni Danegger, PhD

Coni Danegger, PhD, *Sumak Kausay (Good Living) for a flourishing autism. Contexts and meanings of the experience from the Andean Global South*. Salta: Mama Quilla, November 2024.

ISBN 9798346100898

All rights reserved.

Introduction

I live in the northern Andean region of Argentina, in a village that is home to two Kolla indigenous communities: Urkuwasi and Condorwasi. I came here to help raise farm animals for a while, which I managed to combine with working with autistic individuals and continuing to write, late at night and early in the morning, about education and development in autism.

This experience of sharing space and time within the context of indigenous communities open to intercultural exchange and global interaction finally gave meaning and context to echoes of my childhood: my two grandmothers—who have since passed away—came from a rural village whose inhabitants with the same surnames as theirs are now part of the Diaguita-Calchaquí indigenous community.

I had previously had reunions with some of my roots, in several somewhat unexpected displacements, during the long time of the pandemic. Just when, surprisingly, major changes began to coincide in the investigation, understanding, and practices related to autism, especially in the first person, which began to emerge like never before.

I participated fully in this, following my own path of inquiry, understanding, and practices, in various urban and rural contexts, as an autistic woman. These lines are the result of part of what I learned on that journey, as well as teachings from the Q'ero people of Peru.

They contain aspects that could be useful for those who are currently seeking fresh keys for a renewal towards personal development and the well-being of autistic people, following lines that have also been tested over generations.

I share with you here some of the clues of contexts and meanings related to the notion of Sumak Kausay ("good living, good life," in Quechua) that helped me to find myself again now as if returning to and within the wide world of autism and the academic world, and with my peers.

Possibly whoever reads will find some traces of the most current science rediscovering, in its own terms and logic, causes and knowledge lived since ancient times. In this approach I will not refer to categories commonly applied to autism (for example, "disability", "alterations", or even "differences"). Nor will I make a systematic list of practical devices or advice based on these Andean keys.

I leave all of that, and more, for another opportunity. Perhaps to carry it out in minga: as a meeting between Andean thought and that of other regions of the world, among others those of the so-called "Western world." Having a perspective also on the interplanetary human experience, already near.

For a flourishing autism.

CONI DANEGGER
La Caldera, November 2024

THE WORLD AND COSMOS AS A FAMILY

The Andean worldview conceives the world as a family composed of gods, peoples (*ayllus*), *runas*, *warmis*, and *wawas* (men, women, children), and that also encompasses animals, plants, minerals, and entire places, such as mountains (*Apus*). Such diverse family members form a single story that, over time, is continually regenerated and recreated.

In this experience, the planet Earth we are on is part of the cosmos: a family and community with Tayta Inti (the sun), Mama Quilla (the moon), or the Waras (stars) that are part of our daily lives.

These familiar gods, who are mentioned naturally within the Andean world on a daily basis, are not objects of worship, nor are they, for example, in a distant Pantheon.

Beyond the original myths, they are instinctively perceived and named in a practical way as vital elements of existence. They are the earth, the sun, the water, the wind, the fire...

We can talk to them, give them gifts, or ask them for

what we need, and not as supplications, but recognizing their action.

In Andean cultures, people address these gods with closeness and trust, as in a continuous conversation; without formulas or stiffness.

With particular veneration for ancestors, for the elderly.

And to the one who orders everything here: Tayta Inti. And Pachamama, Mother Earth.

Human beings are (only) some of the members of that global, cosmic family.

MOTHER EARTH AS A COMMON HOME

This familiarity with the world is centered and finds its home in Pachamama, Mother Earth.

She is, at the same time, and transcends, every clod of earth and the entire planet Earth.

She is conceived as an entity that embraces and contains each of the beings that are and each of their interactions, providing harmony, development, and encounter.

The cycles of movement and life, which also encompass endings and death, in this understanding, are part of the rhythm of Pachamama, in whom everything finds meaning.

BEING IN FAMILY AND COMMUNITY

The Andean worldview is grounded in concepts that encompass and nuance the ideas of 'family' and 'community' (these words, from Western languages, designate shared visions with cultural differences). In the Andes, it is the *ayllu*.

It is not necessarily identified with the realm of blood family, and in some cases it transcends it. *Ayllu* permeates and signifies diverse forms of relationship, also in a spiritual way and by choice of bonds.

First and foremost, it refers to the person themselves, who is conceived as a community in itself, realizing itself in being and in the development of its various dimensions.

Ayllu is also social and cultural, in reference to other human beings.

This sense of family and of being communal also encompasses the Andean gods, and animals (sacred, domestic, farm or pastoral...), plants, objects (houses, textiles, baskets, vessels...), and also places.

EACH AND EVERYTHING

"Everything is alive," say the *abuelas* and *abuelos* of the Andes.

Everything and every being, forming a whole.

Everything related to everything else.

Within that whole, each being, in its own space-time, as the only and most important thing.

Giving life to the whole.

You too.

And every part of you.

A WORLD WITHOUT WASTE

Pachamama welcomes every being without rejecting any. There is a place for each and every one.

She does not distinguish between convergent or divergent beings. Each of those that are being is unique.

Accepted as it is and as it is being.

Every species, every person, animal or plant, and even every fruit, every leaf. Every stone, big or small. Every grain of sand, dune and mountain.

At the same time, every being is being in motion, within some form of change.

In the changes that involve the seasons of the year, or of life.

In every change of the moon, every menstrual cycle, every change of cycle.

In every sprout and every wound.

Every apparent mistake, break, loss, death or new beginning.

No being or life is waste or wasted.

Each and every one is valuable and necessary.

No stretch of the *ayllu's* life, nor that of anything or anyone, is wasted.

Under the rain and then when the sun comes out, and the small leaves or dry branches that have fallen from the trees lie on the ground. For Pachamama they are part of the cycle of life, renewing themselves as they transmute into humus, roots, trunk, leaves, flowers, fruits.

DIMENSIONS OF EXISTENCE

Human existence, like the Andes, has dimensions that are conceived spatially and in relation to forms of life. Personal lives unfold in the *kay pacha*, which is this world we see and inhabit.

At the same time, in relation to a world conceived as superior and broader, whose characteristic animals fly or are lighter: it is the *hanaj pacha*.

Another dimension of their existence is linked to the underworld, the *urku pacha*, populated by a variety of characters and myths.

These worlds coexist and interact in the subjectivities of people in the Andes, forming part of their personal journey of self-knowledge and self-acceptance.

STARTING OVER

Andean time is cyclical.

It renews itself by repeating milestones, around the reiterations of Pachamama: in the seasons of the year, the movements of the sun, the constellations, the moon.

It indicates time for everything, like nature.

Times for work, for celebration, for resting, for letting things rest.

Time to save the seed and time to sow, time for the first harvest and for the great harvest.

All times have meaning: their periods of rapid change, pruning or storms, their moments of waiting, their apparent slowness.

In this, each being carries its own rhythm, which is observed and respected by ancestral wisdom.

With the mark of renewed opportunities to start over.

COMPLEMENTS

Andean culture has no fondness for arbitrariness without vital meaning.

For example, for reasons of external aesthetics or for show, "so that onlookers can see."

Pachamama is authentic.

For her, a rose in bloom is not inherently better than the humus that contributed to and is part of the rose's fullness.

That same rose will be humus, in another space-time.

Also in fullness.

Similarly, it recognizes two energies that are distinguished and equally valued: one energy is refined (*sami*) and the other, dense (*hucha*).

Refined energy is not better than dense energy: it is different. It corresponds to certain situations or conditions.

The dense energy is also valid, needed, complementary for continuity of the life.

HARMONY AND HARMONIZING

Likewise, some directions of action are to harmonize.

The acceptance of what is being leads, in the matrix of Pachamama, to seek or make progress in its harmony, with itself and with the rest.

The notion of everything and diverse implies movement, space-times and rites of harmonization, as part of the path towards *Sumak Kausay*.

Changing or restoring disposition, order or form, towards that which fulfills and realizes each being, while it is being.

Without leaving in this each one of being what it is.

Also *sami*, the refined energy, may need to be harmonized.

Hucha too, and it would continue to be dense energy, although harmonized.

PURIFYING

Along the way we get dirty, we accumulate, we lose clarity.

To harmonize, before acting by filling or remedying, the Andean culture pauses, observes and cleans.

Not to leave impeccable, perfect or harmless, but to return to the origin and renew, starting cycles again.

There are many Andean rites, and also special days of the year, dedicated to purification, cleaning or *pampachay*.

Of houses, bodies, thoughts, intentions, objects.

To the flow of Mama Cocha, the sacred mother of water, and often with the participation of Tayta Inti (the sun), Mama Quilla (the moon), or Tayta Huayra (the wind).

With the help of herbs, flowers or roots of sacred plants or domestic cultivation. With salt. Sometimes, with earth. With incense. With chants and invocations. With washing machines, soaps, brooms and dusters.

Sometimes, with the help of people who are specialists in specific matters.

Counting on it now, with the help of sciences and professions.

Usually, in a personal way, based on the observation and understanding of oneself in interaction with the elements of nature. Paying attention to the clues of ancestral wisdom.

NOURISHING AND HEALING

Pachamama, nature, is the one who heals, who restores balance.

The Andean worldview conceives that disharmony and discomfort affect not only people, but also their environments (their houses or places), and also nature.

Therefore, harmonizing must also be done in those other areas.

Ordinarily, people administer their own *hampis*, medicine chests with healing herbs.

Food also has functions of medicine, to nourish, prevent or cure.

Communities entrust some tasks, spiritual and healing, to traditional medicine, to their *yatiris*.

Their action and form of preparation is transmitted from one generation to another, as part of the initiation into the *runa warmi*, the moments of life.

ATTACHMENT AND NURTURING

Andean families don't typically experience the sense of exclusive possession or belonging of their children that is characteristic of Western cultures.

Rather, there is, on the one hand, the perception that las *wawas*, children, are particularly connected to the mysterious world of the gods, especially Pachamama, the loving Mother Earth.

On the other hand, they belong to the ayllu. In fact, aspects of child-rearing are done communally, amidst the rounds of *comadres*.

The supervision of grandmothers takes into account ancestral wisdom to interpret signs and indicate what to do in the different situations of the community's children.

Likewise, Andean mothers, and sometimes fathers, are often recognized because they carry their *qepi* (a woolen cloth) on their backs, carrying, wrapped and bundled, a baby or a small child.

From this relationship of closeness at the beginning of their lives, Andean children are initiated into the participation of the life, times and activities of the *ayllu*, while at the same time constructing a vision of the world from bonds of attachment.

With the first haircut, around the age of three, comes their first milestone of autonomy, celebrated with great fanfare and a community feast.

ACCOMPANYING, PARTICIPATING, PRACTICING

Andean culture educates through presence, accompaniment, and practice, not through explicit teaching.

Accompaniment is first from the children, assisting and witnessing every step, action, and exchange. Then, with their curiosity and autonomous action, observing and asking the elders.

Afterwards, practicing.

There, the presence that is education is transformed into that of the one who observes, asks, encourages, guides them.

In a close or remote way, when the young people of the ayllu are initiated into more advanced forms, according to the passage of time.

With progressively greater autonomy: from being a helper in household chores to being responsible for tasks of increasing importance; until later being able to carry out many and all tasks autonomously outside the home.

Later forming, towards adolescence, a home of their own, as a kind of test.

Also testing the relationships of choice and formation of their own family, through *sirviñaco*.

With the accompaniment of ancestors, grandparents of the *ayllu* and all their wisdom.

And the cycle begins again.

SOLITUDE, SENSE OF SELF AND AUTONOMY

The experience of being alone for hours, days or weeks is a common experience in the mountains, from childhood or adolescence.

It implies taking care of oneself and being good company for oneself, building and nourishing the intimacy of their own *ayllu*, all one and diverse, personal.

Also developing autonomously in daily household chores and work.

Caring for and moving grazing animals, or being in charge of shearing them.

Planning and carrying out medium and long-term tasks, such as sowing and cultivation calendars.

Contributing to the continuous construction of the house - as a living being that it is.

Dedicating oneself to the making of textiles, preserves, tanning, for own use or for exchange.

Attending to the interiority of an eloquent, assertive and confident voice.

Remembering knowledge and stories and preserving new memories to share back in the community.

Those who are alone in this way continue to be part of the community.

RECOGNIZING ONE'S OWN EXPERIENCE

As the year progresses, daily customs are renewed, and with them also festivals.

In some cases, coinciding with what is most useful or convenient, or with the availability of what exists.

Thus, for example, there are winter and summer meals, with different nutritional properties and according to the foods that are produced at that time.

But also recognizing how the interaction of the world makes us experience and experience ourselves.

In community, for example, recognizing, validating and making a rite and a feast of the variety of emotions, sensations or moods that occur in the year of the *ayllu*.

Thus, accompanying the vital rhythms of the times of the year, there are, for example, instruments and ways of making music. In winter, in a more serious, sad and melancholic way; in summer, more acute, lively and festive. The *caja bagualera*, a reflection and vehicle of expression of Andean subjectivity, has, for example, these two forms and uses.

SILENCE AND MYSTERY

Andean silence is outlined against the sounds of life, in mountains, valleys, plateaus, ravines, and plains.

The Andean worldview particularly respects and values this silence - as well as, in its spaces and times, the exchange of words or couplets, laughter, and the noise of celebration and festivity.

The peculiar silence of the Andean people is not a sign of emptiness, ignorance, or disdain.

It is lived as an experience and realm of intimacy and openness to listening.

Also, a context of contemplation and discovery of mystery.

GREETING

The act of greeting is particularly revered in the Andean world.

Perhaps favored by the circumstance that it is frequent to travel long distances, often walking or riding animals, or that some communities are transhumant.

Words of greeting are not mere passing formalities or empty formulas.

Often people have preferred words, chosen carefully, to express their greeting as a form of blessing.

There are traditional greetings that reveal desires, intentions, or common codes of conduct:

> "*Ama sua*: do not be a thief.
> *Ama llulla*: do not be a liar.
> *Ama quella*: do not be lazy."

MUSIC AND DANCE

The Andean worldview is expressed in the languages of music and dance as systems of knowledge, communication, and social exchange.

Dance, an occasion for celebration, encounter, and rest, is ritualistic and based on various familiar rhythms and harmonies.

Music is listened to and also made, communally. It is part of daily experience as an accepted form of communication of one's own feelings, desires, and thoughts.

For example, in singing with the *caja*, individually, in a circle of *comadres* or *compadres*, or with the grace and spark of counterpoint and competition in improvisation.

They involve learning and training, which are highly valued in communities.

PAGO AND GIFT

August 1st is a purification feast in the Andean world: the month of Pachamama begins.

In every home, a vigorous cleaning is carried out, sometimes general. From early on, the smoke of burning obsolete objects can be seen, as well as incense (*sahumar*).

On August 2nd, the loving celebration ceremonies usually begin, which are in the manner of a 'payment' (*pago*) to Mother Earth.

Everywhere, people gather around an excavation in the earth, usually made the previous year and the year before.

Each time, first to see if Pacha has consumed all the offering of the previous year: it would be a good omen to find nothing of it.

Meanwhile, the people present are preparing to make their donation. Inside, remembering their reasons for giving thanks and their new requests.

Outside, with plant incense and prayers.

To the sound of music and murmuring, people pass the offering in pairs, with the help of those who have prepared and invited to the ceremony.

Generously, they give Mother Earth drinks and food. Everything that is pleasing to people must be shared with her.

Water, juices, coca-cola, beer, wines and liquors, richly prepared foods, sweets, desserts, precious seeds... Also cigarettes and coca leaves, sacred under the protection of Mama Kuka.

All this, while the people around continue their usual conversations, the children continue to play, the domestic animals come and go.

Pachamama and the offering are part of everyday domestic life.

RECIPROCITY

Ayni is one of the Andean names for reciprocity in giving, donating, offering.

In the balance and equilibrium of the *ayllu*, this has both material and spiritual dimensions.

It is not conceived that there are people who only receive, or only give.

Everyone can contribute something.

Everyone can and should receive retribution.

In different ways: with the exchange of objects or actions, such as barter or swapping, or money.

Pachamama also gives and receives.

To the rites of *pago* is sometimes added, especially in festive times:

> *¡Pachamama, kusilla kusilla!*
> Pachamama, be propitious.
> Be generous in your gift.

A WISE AND KNOWING BODY

The *pocpo* (body) is the one who knows. Andean wisdom does not conceive that one can know with only or primarily with one part, for example the brain.

The consideration of "the cognitive" as detached from the body would be foreign to this worldview.

Beyond neurocentrism, it is conceived that each body knows with its various vital systems, in its relationship with the world.

The different areas of the body have particular qualities for exploring and knowing. Each one looks and sees, literally, from their own *ñawis*, or eyes, which are the organ of knowledge of that area of the *pocpo*.

The notions of 'knowing' and 'living' become inseparable in an Andean word to designate knowledge: *yachay*.

In this conception, the body knows through its practical action, which is doing, as well as perception, intuition, and creation.

The body carries within it traces of what ancestors have known.

Also what past stories and events have deposited in its memory, signified by one's own life experience.

UNITY AND DIVERSITY

In Pachamama, the whole is one.

Within that fundamental one, all the diversity of existence is found.

The one is the fullness of the diverse.

The diverse fulfills the one and only.

In every being that is, that is being.

Also, with respect to the community, everything that is unity of all diversities.

That welcomes and forms unity in the diversity of the diverse.

With all its ways of being, and its intersections.

NO NEED FOR INCLUSION

In Pachamama, each one is part of the whole. Not as a belonging, but as a part.

Nature does not need to include: it simply is, in unity and diversity.

For the Andean intuition, everything is already included, so to speak.

The notion of 'including', as an action verb, or 'being included' as a condition or situation of an object, makes no sense from this perspective.

Who could presume to allow or make room (or not), alongside themselves, as equals, for other human beings, to 'include' them.

Perhaps unconsciously they would have had to displace those equals, even in their own thoughts.

Those pairs were already being. Without aspects of their diversity, or their trajectory in time, for example, conditioning or being an obstacle to their being *ayllu*.

In the Andean worldview, inclusion is taken for granted, it is implicit in *ayllu*.

SUMAK KAUSAY AND PERSONAL DEVELOPMENT

Sumak Kausay goes beyond the concept of "being happy".

Sumak is fullness, realization.

Kausay, life, and also movement.

It channels the notion of well-being, with a nuance.

Always in movement, in vital dynamism, the well-being of the Andean worldview is good-being.

Becoming.

Never finished, complete or closed.

It is also translated as "good life" and "good living": with meaning and purpose, careful, shared, useful, worked; and also enjoyable, graceful, and grateful.

Sumak Kausay is a vital path, *ñan*, traveled with a sense of global, universal community, but in a personal and practical way.

Again and again, like the cycles of Pachamama, starting over.

EPILOGUE

Under the protection of Pachamama, autism can be an opportunity to take a somewhat different path than those known in other cultures of the world.

In some aspects, possibly more delicately appropriate and respectful.

I wish for you that knowledge of the Andean world inspires ways and times of renewal.